Pizza Counting

By Christina Dobson

Illustrated by
Matthew Holmes

i⌂i Charlesbridge

If you think pizza is delicious, say "Delizioso!" That's how people say "Delicious!" in Italy where the first pizza was made. This is a plain cheese pizza. It has zero pieces on top. It has only crust, cheese, and tomato sauce.

The first pizza had no sauce because there were no tomatoes. Explorers brought the first tomato seeds from America to Europe in the 1500s. For the next two hundred years, most people thought tomatoes were poisonous.

1

2

Let's face it — a tasty pizza will put a smile on the face of any hungry kid. A plain pizza is like a blank piece of paper — a great place to create a picture. The picture on this pizza is made from one mushroom, two olives, three strips of green bell pepper, and four slices of tomato.

4

3

Bell peppers come in five colors: green, yellow, orange, red, and purple. Would you like to be a purple pepper eater?

4

1 + 2 = 3

2 + 3 = 5

3 + 4 = 7

1 + 3 = 4

5

6

You could celebrate the Fourth of July with this patriotic pizza. Its flag design is made of five eggplant stars, six red onion strips, seven cheese stripes, and eight red pepper pieces.

8

7

Pizza has become as American as apple pie. There are more than 60,000 pizza restaurants in the United States.

6

5 + 6 = 11

6 + 8 = 14

7 + 8 = 15

5 + 7 = 12

7

9

10

Once upon a time, people decided that pizza was the perfect snack food. It's a tasty, quick meal, especially if it is a clock pizza with nine green pepper pieces, ten tiny meatballs, eleven red onion strips, and twelve salami slices.

11

12

It takes only ten minutes to bake a pizza in a very hot oven of about 550°. In Italy, the bakers sometimes used red-hot volcanic rocks to heat their pizza ovens.

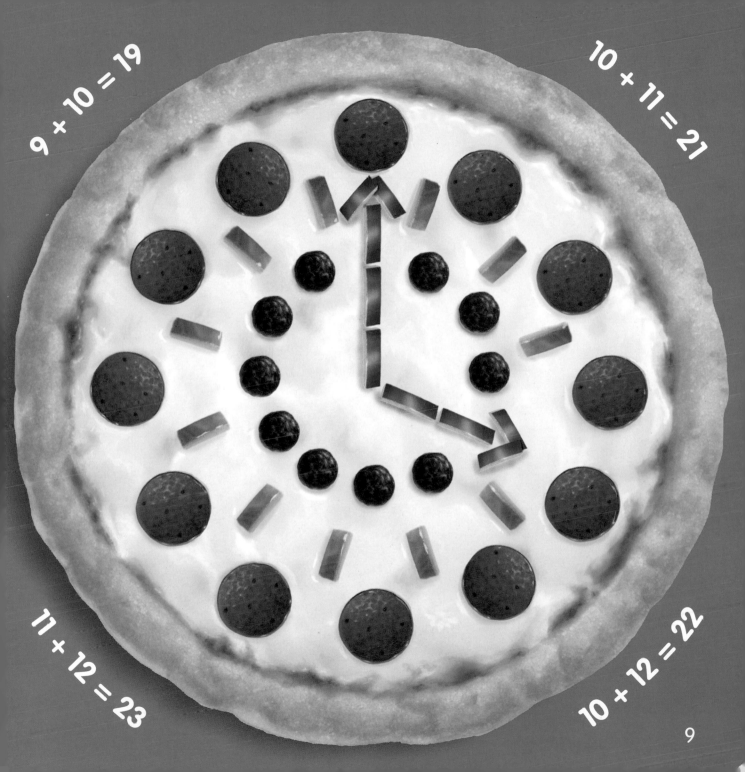

9 + 10 = 19

10 + 11 = 21

11 + 12 = 23

10 + 12 = 22

13

14

When a surprise is discovered too soon, we say the cat is out of the bag. This cat is out of a box — a pizza box. Would it surprise you to discover a cat pizza with 13 onion strips, 14 chive pieces, 15 pepperoni slices, and 16 basil leaves?

15

16

Some pizzas make a purrfect dessert. They have jam instead of tomato sauce, and pieces of fruit on top.

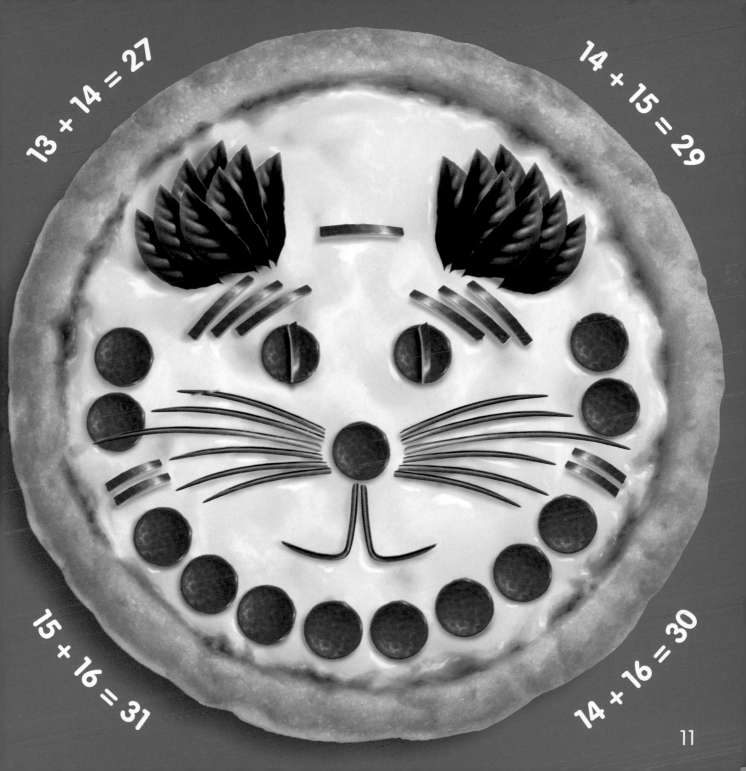

13 + 14 = 27

14 + 15 = 29

15 + 16 = 31

14 + 16 = 30

17

18

People all over the world eat pizza. In some places, people like tuna, coconut, bean sprouts, or pickled ginger on their pizzas. Would you like this planet Earth pizza with 17 strips of green bell pepper, 18 chive pieces, 19 pepperoni slices, and 20 onion strips?

19

20

The largest pizza ever made was 140 feet across.

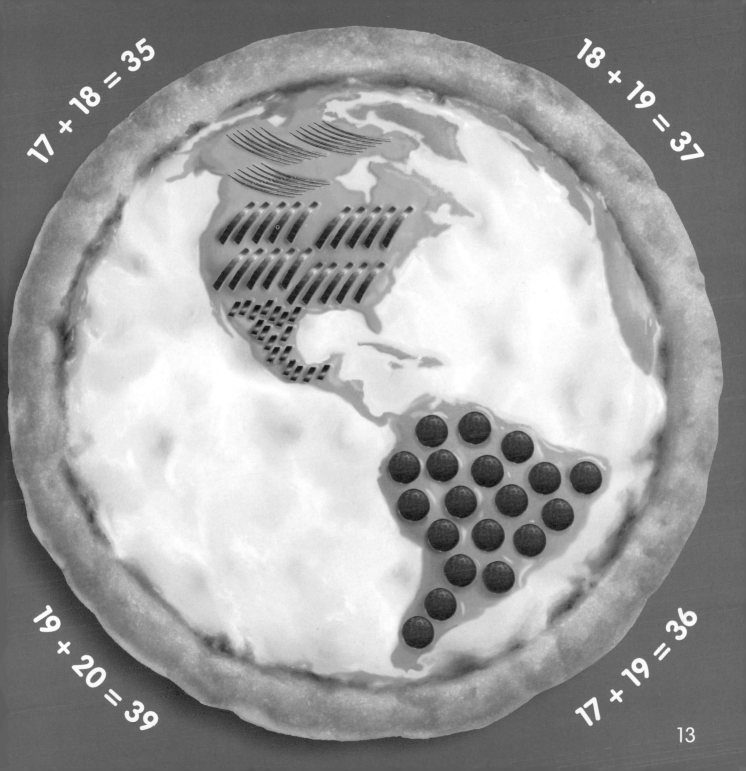

17 + 18 = 35

18 + 19 = 37

19 + 20 = 39

17 + 19 = 36

This pizza has 100 pieces on top.

Is that 20 pieces each of 5 different kinds?

$$
\begin{array}{r}
20 \\
20 \\
20 \\
20 \\
+20 \\
\hline
100
\end{array}
\qquad
\begin{array}{r}
20 \\
\times\ 5 \\
\hline
100
\end{array}
$$

Maybe it is 10 pieces each of 10 different kinds.

$$
\begin{array}{r}
10 \\
10 \\
10 \\
10 \\
10 \\
10 \\
10 \\
10 \\
10 \\
+10 \\
\hline
100
\end{array}
\qquad
\begin{array}{r}
10 \\
\times 10 \\
\hline
100
\end{array}
$$

Or is it 25 pieces each of 4 different kinds?

$$
\begin{array}{r}
25 \\
\times\ 4 \\
\hline
100
\end{array}
\qquad
\begin{array}{r}
25 \\
25 \\
25 \\
+25 \\
\hline
100
\end{array}
$$

Any way you look at it, it adds up to a total of 100 pieces on top of this super-giganto-mega pizza!

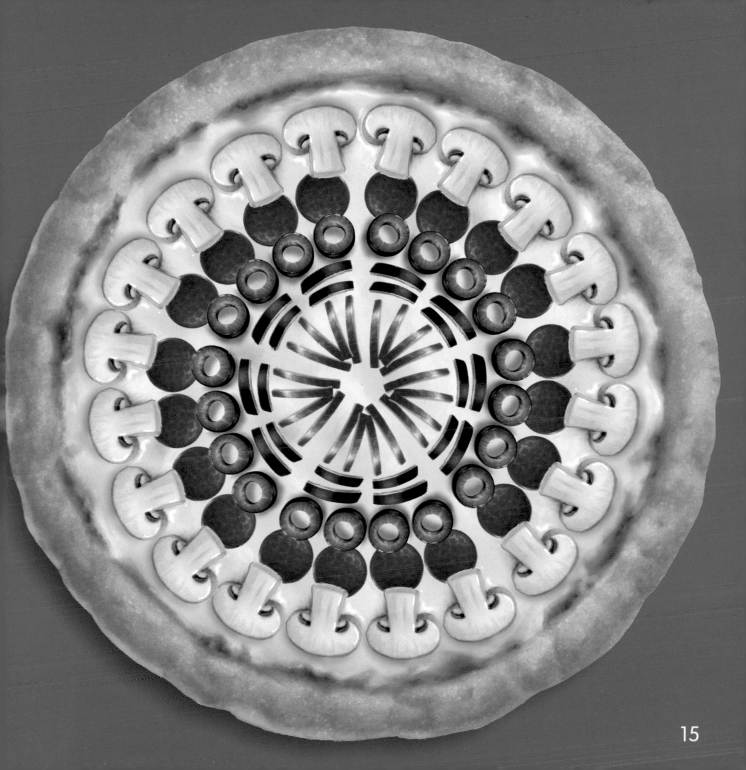

If you were throwing a pizza party for a giant, you might make ten of these super-giganto-mega-pizzas, with 100 pieces on top of each. How many total pieces would that be?

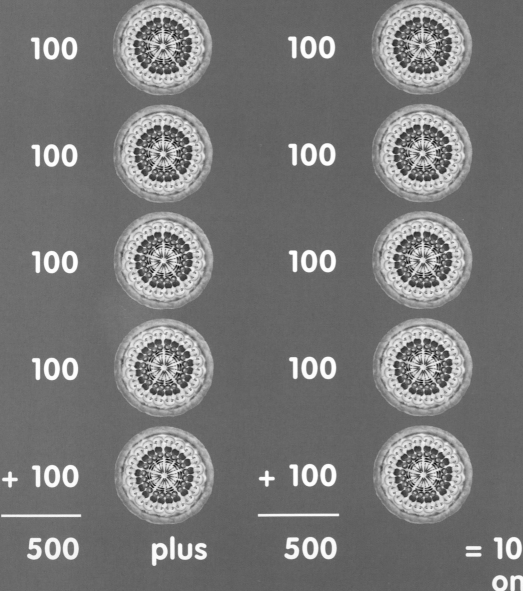

100 · 100

100 · 100

100 · 100

100 · 100

+ 100 · + 100

500 · plus · 500 · = 1000 pieces on top

If you had a really big party, you might need 100 pizzas with 100 pieces on each. How many pieces would you need in total?

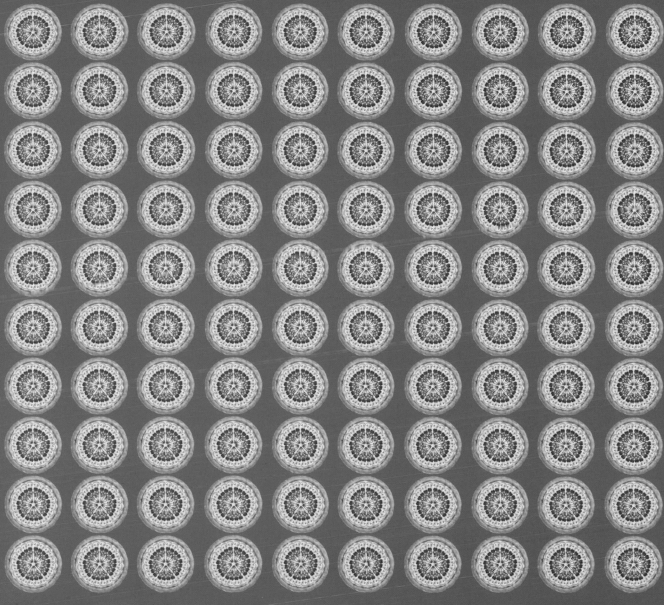

100 x 100 = 10,000 pieces on top

It would take more than 131,000,000
twelve-inch pizzas to circle the
Earth at the equator.

131,000,000

One hundred thirty-one million

That's a lot of pizza, but we eat even more than one hundred thirty-one million pizzas each year in America.

You would need more than 1,260,000,000 twelve-inch pizzas

placed crust to crust to build a pizza path to the moon.

1,260,000,000

One billion
two hundred sixty million

Americans eat more than enough pizza to reach the moon.
All of us together eat over 2,375,000,000 pizzas each year.

All this talk about pizza could make you hungry. You could cut a pizza in half so it has two equal parts. If you have a whale of an appetite, you might eat half a pizza.

Anchovy pizzas are the least popular with people, but whales might like them. A whale can eat a ton of anchovies a day. That's 2,000 pounds, which is enough to make about 16,000 anchovy pizzas.

A pizza that is cut into three equal slices is divided into thirds. The triceratops had three horns on its head, and this triceratops pizza has three pieces.

Perhaps the triceratops became extinct because it didn't eat healthy foods. Pizza is a healthy food with lots of protein, carbohydrates, vitamins, and calcium.

A pizza that is cut into four equal slices is divided into fourths. You'd be really lucky to find this four-leaf-clover pizza for dinner.

For a green pizza sauce, some people like pesto, which is usually made of basil leaves, olive oil, grated cheese, pine nuts, and garlic.

A pizza that is cut into five equal slices is divided into fifths. Would you buy this nickel pizza for five cents?

Pizza used to cost a nickel a slice, but now it costs 30 times as much. Even at today's prices, pizza is a good value.

A pizza that is cut into six equal slices is divided into sixths. To share this target pizza with two friends, you could aim for two pieces each.

Pizza chefs need good aim. Some pizza makers flip the dough up into the air. As it spins, the dough stretches out from the center into a thin circle.

A pizza that is cut into eight equal slices is divided into eighths. If you eat four eighths of this flower pizza, you will still have one half left.

Pizza crust is made of yeast, salt, water, and flour — not flower.

This train pizza is divided into tenths. If you ate two slices each day, it would last for five days. If you're really hungry, you could eat five slices for two days — chew, chew!

The first pizza delivery was to a queen! When Queen Margherita of Savoy visited Naples, she ordered the baker to bring her pizza. Today, you can order pizza on the telephone or over the Internet.

This calendar pizza is divided into twelfths. The year is divided into twelve months. If you eat three pieces, you could eat an entire summer, winter, fall, or spring!

October is National Pizza Month, but any day of the year is a good day to celebrate with pizza.

Now think about being really hungry for pizza. Which size slice would you rather have?

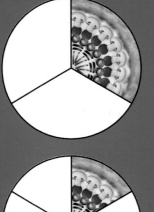

one third or one fourth?

⅓ or ¼?

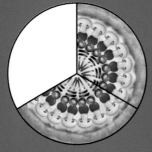

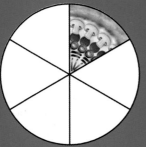

one sixth or one eighth?

⅙ or ⅛?

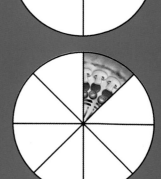

two thirds or two sixths?

⅔ or ²/₆?

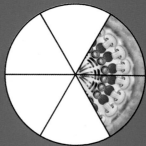

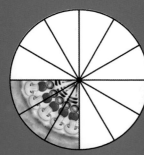

three twelfths or one fourth?

³/₁₂ or ¼?

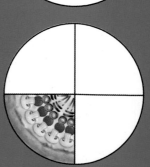

Pizza Fractions

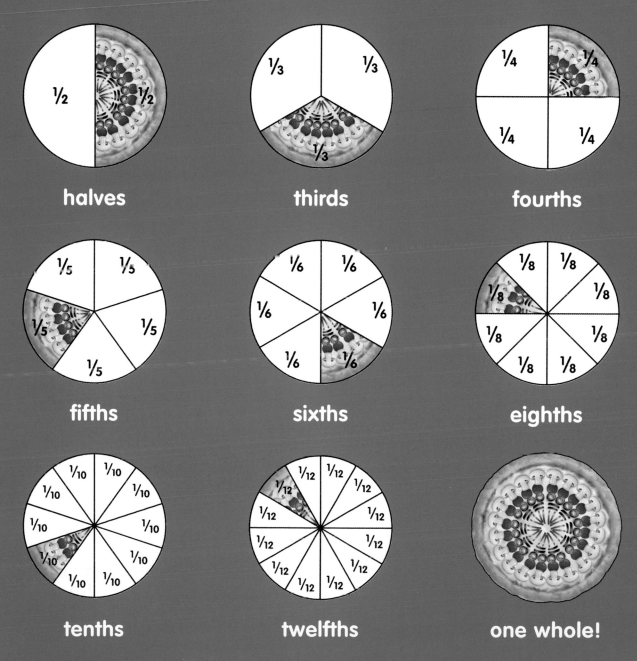

halves

thirds

fourths

fifths

sixths

eighths

tenths

twelfths

one whole!

To my husband Dave who counts on pizza at least
once a week — C.D.

To Megan and Lauren, with love . . . and pepperoni,
hold the anchovies — M.H.

Text copyright © 2003 by Christina Dobson
Illustration copyright © 2003 by Matthew Holmes

Published by Charlesbridge, 85 Main Street, Watertown, MA 02472
(617) 926-0329 • www.charlesbridge.com

Library of Congress Cataloging-in-Publication Data
Dobson, Christina.
    The pizza counting book / by Christina Dobson : illustrated by Matthew Holmes.
        p. cm.
Summary: Decorated pizzas are used to introduce counting and fractions.
Includes facts about pizza.
ISBN 978-0-88106-338-7 (reinforced for library use)
ISBN 978-0-88106-339-4 (softcover)
ISBN 978-1-60734-291-5 (ebook pdf)
1. Counting—Juvenile literature. 2. Pizza—Juvenile literature.
[1. Counting. 2. Fractions. 3. Pizza.] I. Holmes, Matthew, ill. II. Title.
    QA113 .D63 2002
    513.2'11—dc21   2002002381

Printed by Sung In Printing in Gunpo-Si, Kyonggi-Do, Korea
(hc) 10 9 8 7 6 5 4 3
(sc) 10